A Mark Dahle Portfolio

Connected

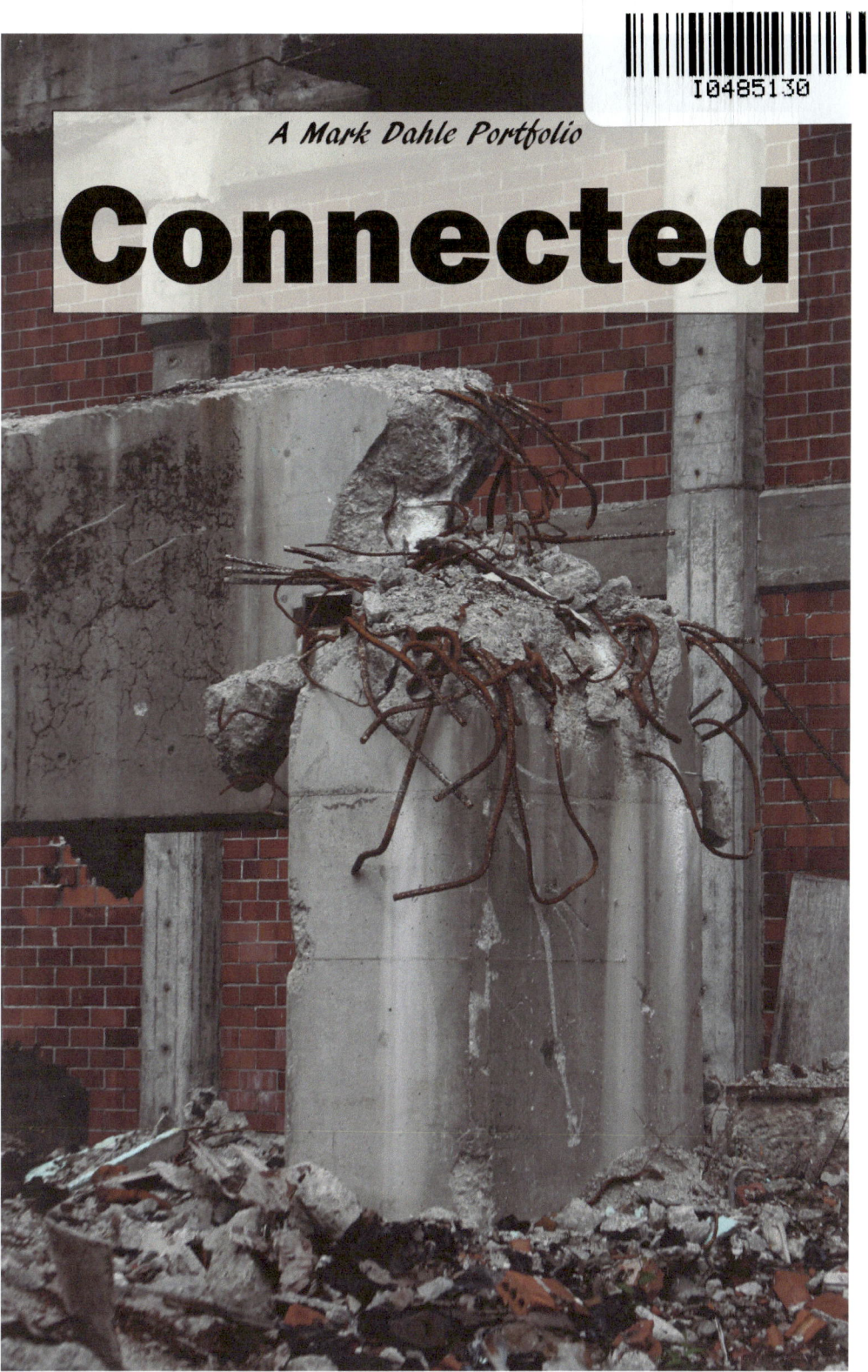

Mark Dahle Portfolios can be read in a few minutes and enjoyed for a lifetime.

This portfolio includes a commentary about how connected people and animals are, a photo of a beautiful 36 x 24 inch painting (at the right) and twenty-five outstanding photographs from Ketchikan, Alaska.

Unlike many picture books, the text is unrelated to the paintings and photographs. This might seem weird at first. One thing that helps is to order more portfolios until you get used to it.

Photographs in this book are available in limited editions. See http://www.MarkDahle.com for more information and for previews of upcoming portfolios.

We do our best to create portfolios free of editing mistakes. But if we miss anything, we reward people who report errors. For details see MarkDahle.com/Typos.html or email MarkDahle@aol.com with the subject line "Typos."

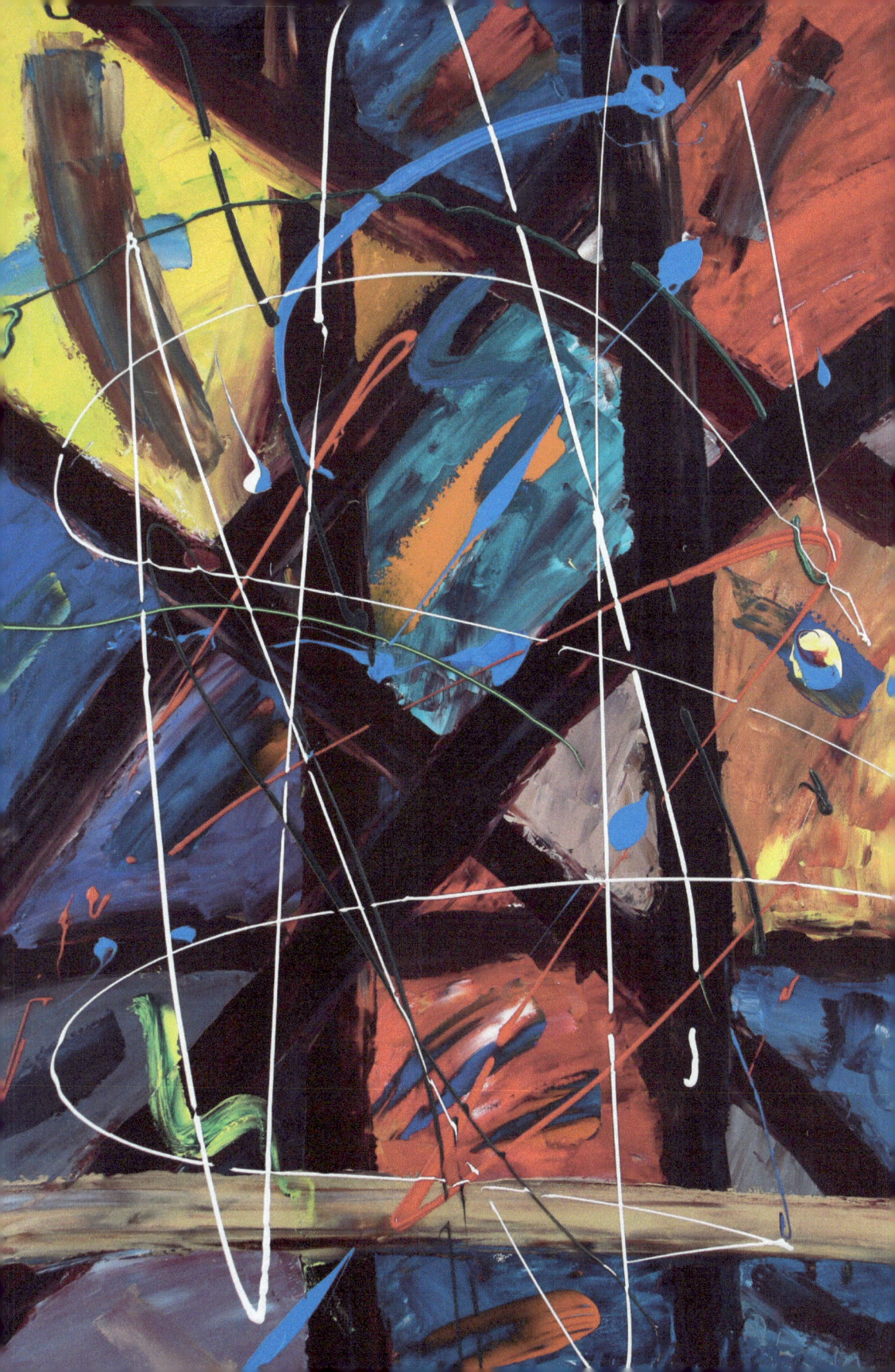

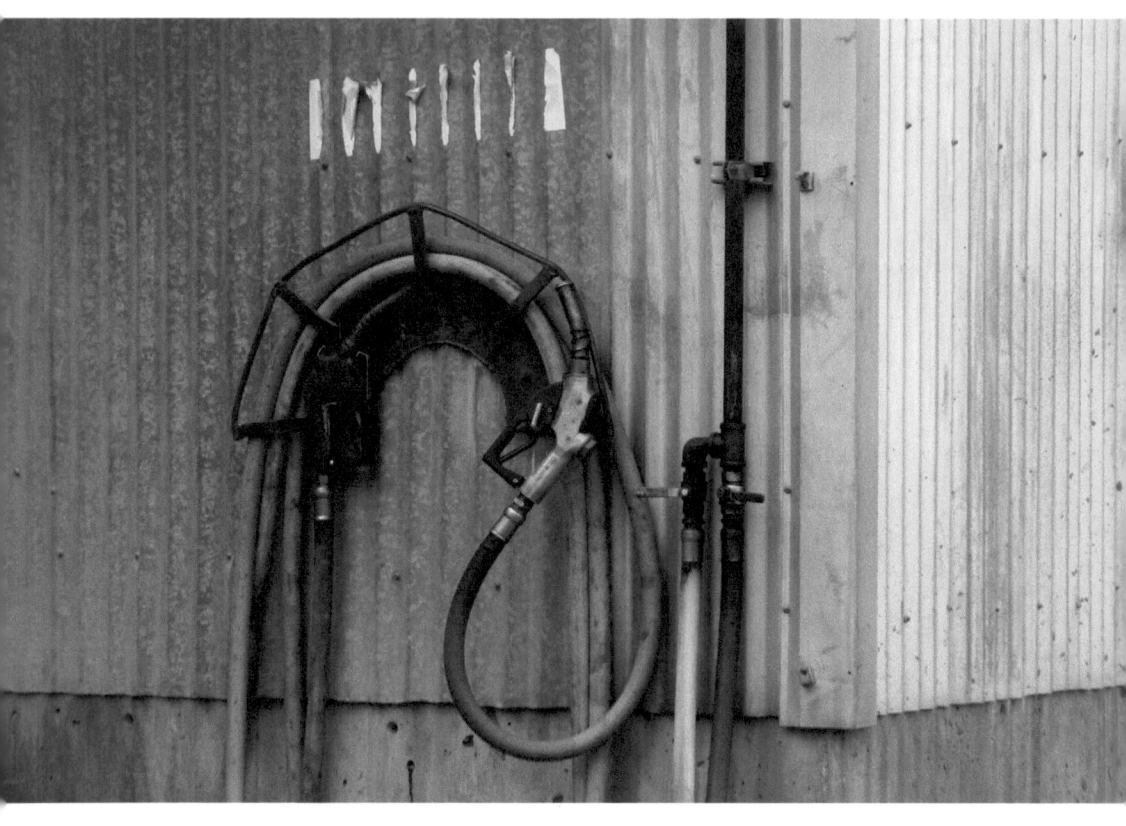

Several years ago I rented a cabin on a lake. One of the windows in the cabin had a curtain that was always closed.

A tree was outside the window. One year a mother robin chose the tree as the place for her nest, and she put her nest right beside the window.

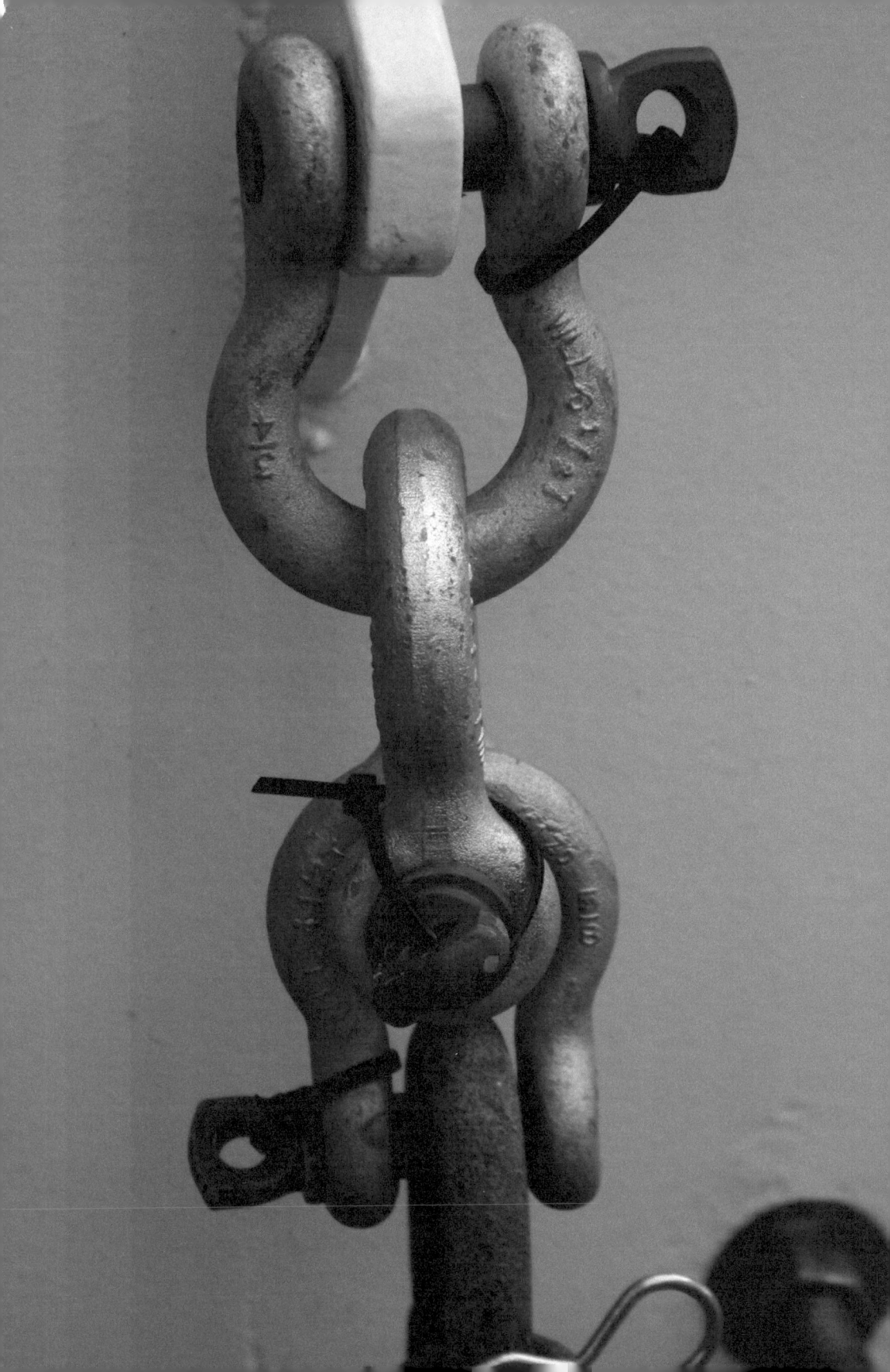

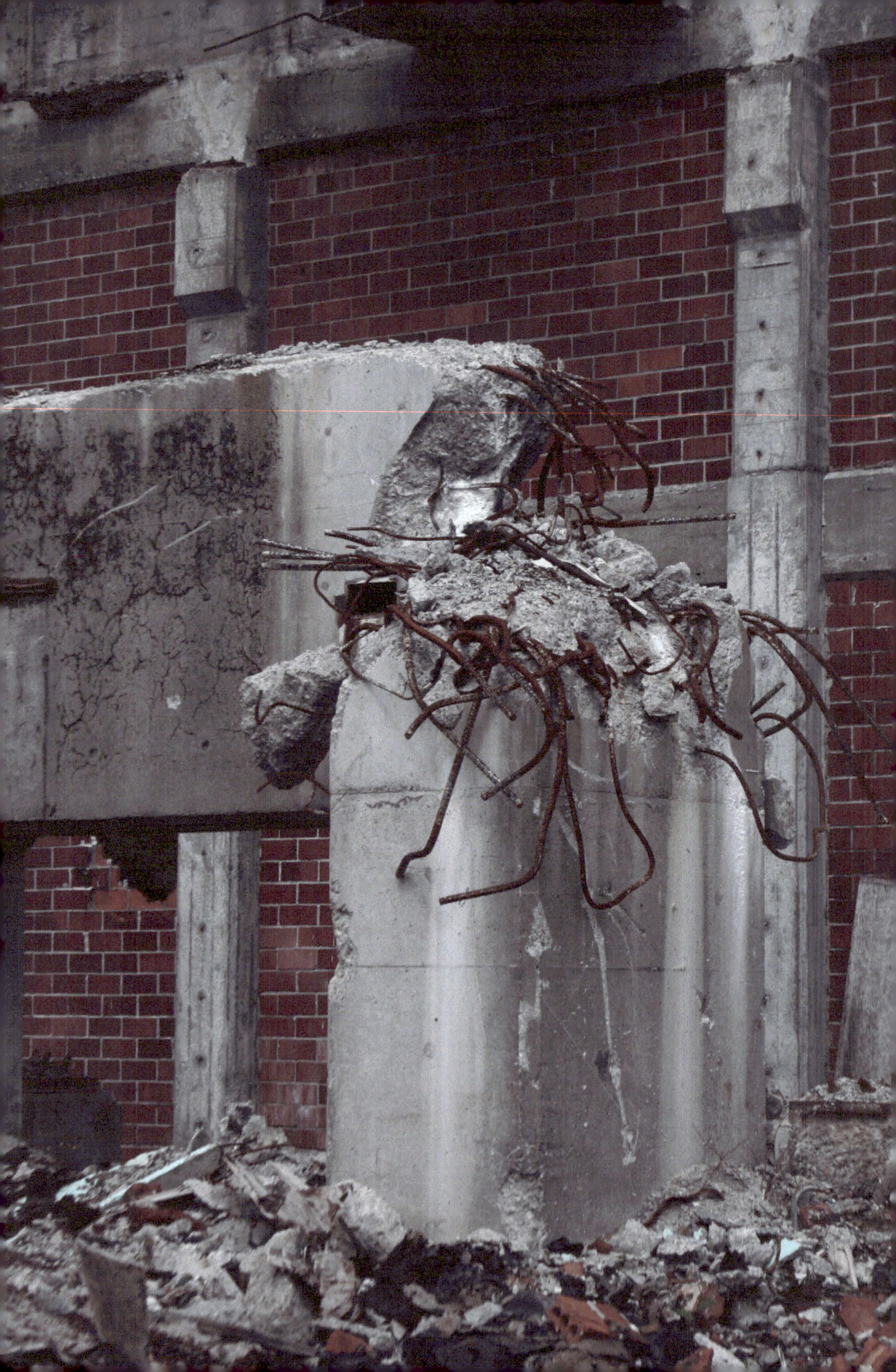

When I discovered it, I set up a camera on a tripod next to the curtain. For about two minutes a day I took pictures of the mom and her nest and her eggs – and eventually of the baby robins as they grew.

At first the mother robin didn't notice. I would pull the curtain back just enough so the lens was peeking out, take a couple pictures, and then put everything back. Once she noticed, however, she was quite unhappy for those two minutes each day.

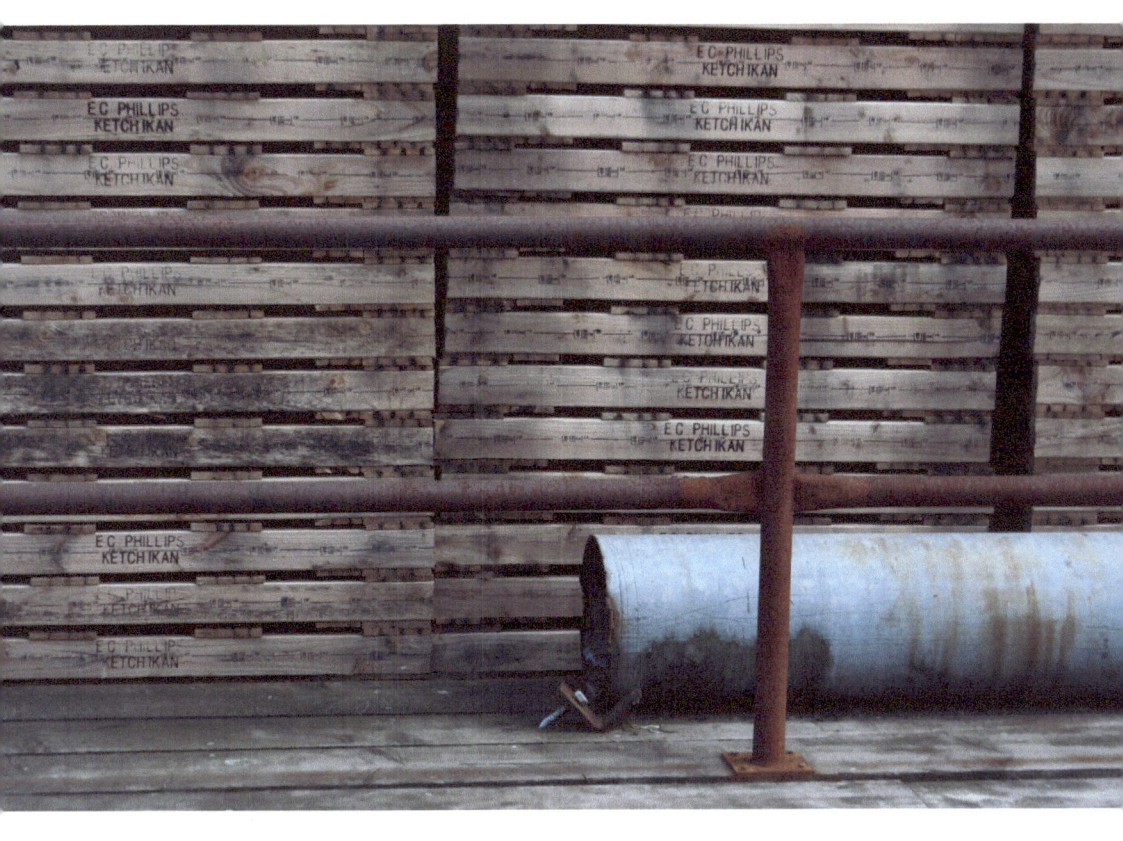

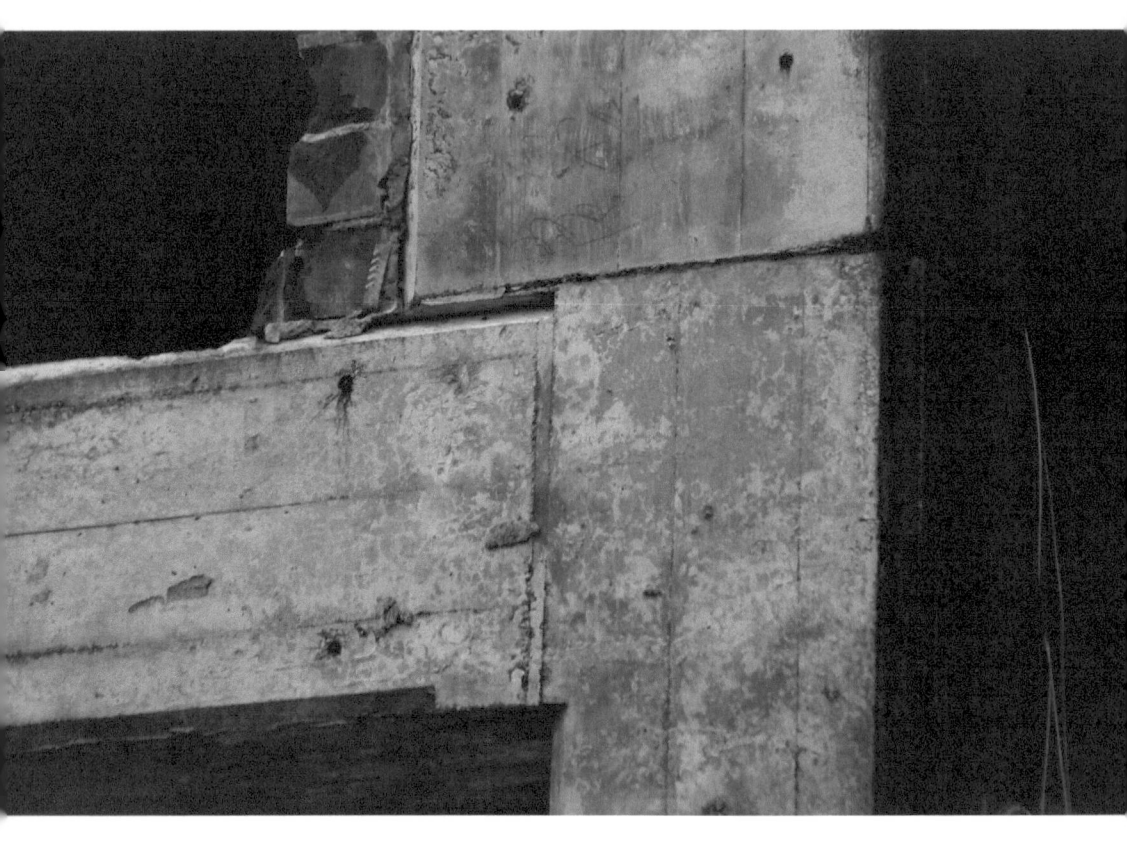

Before spending time with the robin and her eggs, I didn't know that robins have a variety of calls. I hadn't paid attention. But over the course of a week or two, I got to know several different calls of the robin, including her distress call.

When the baby robins hatched, I kept taking pictures of them as they grew, a couple minutes a day.

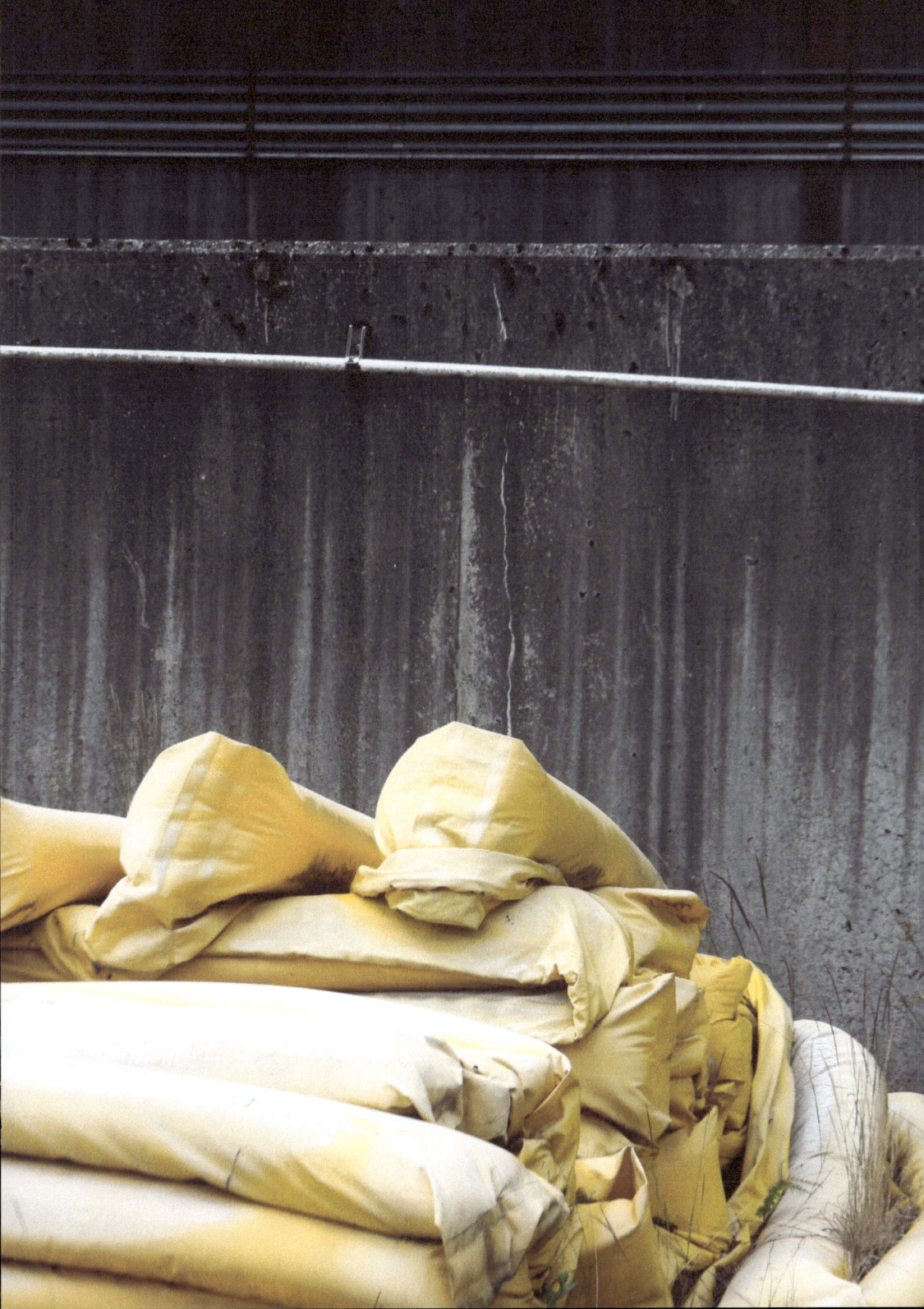

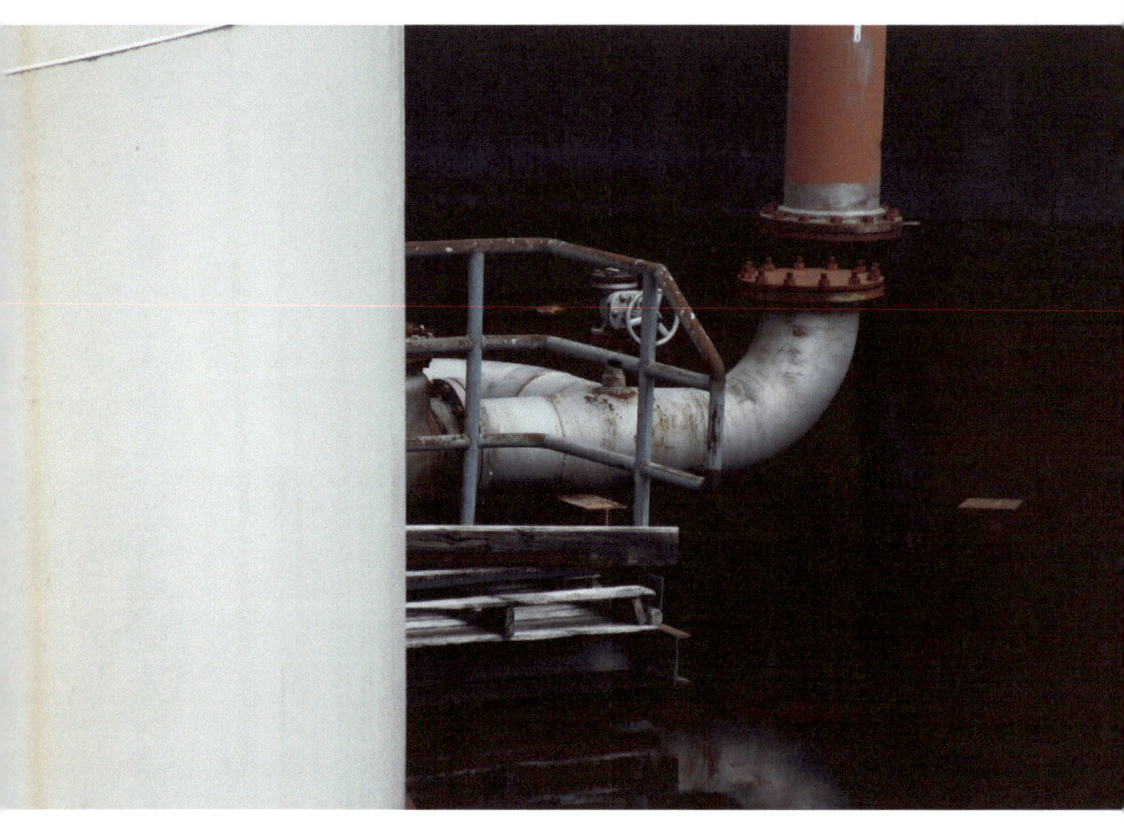

One night about 3 a.m. I awoke to the sound of the robin's distress call. I made up my mind not to get up. I wanted to sleep. It couldn't be that important. Besides, it was 3 a.m.

"I'm not getting up," I thought. "The only thing that could make me get up was if that robin flew around the cabin."

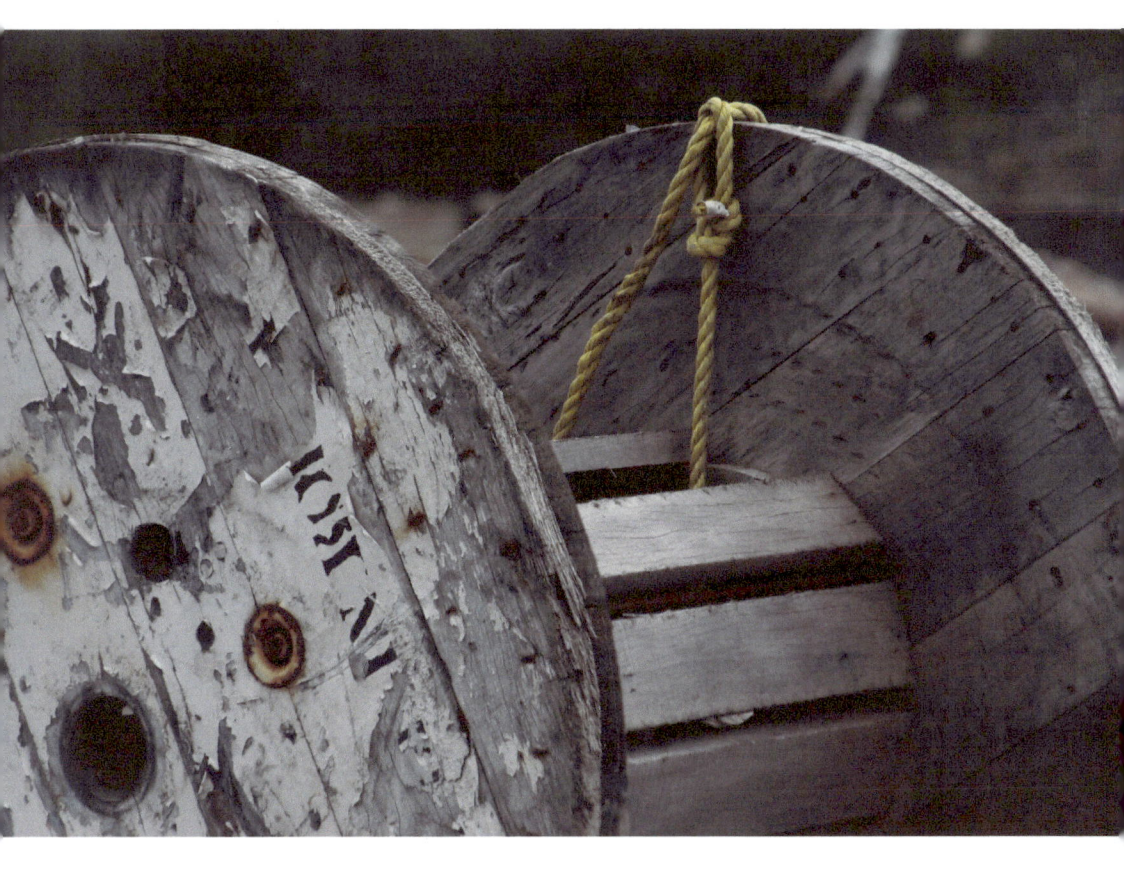

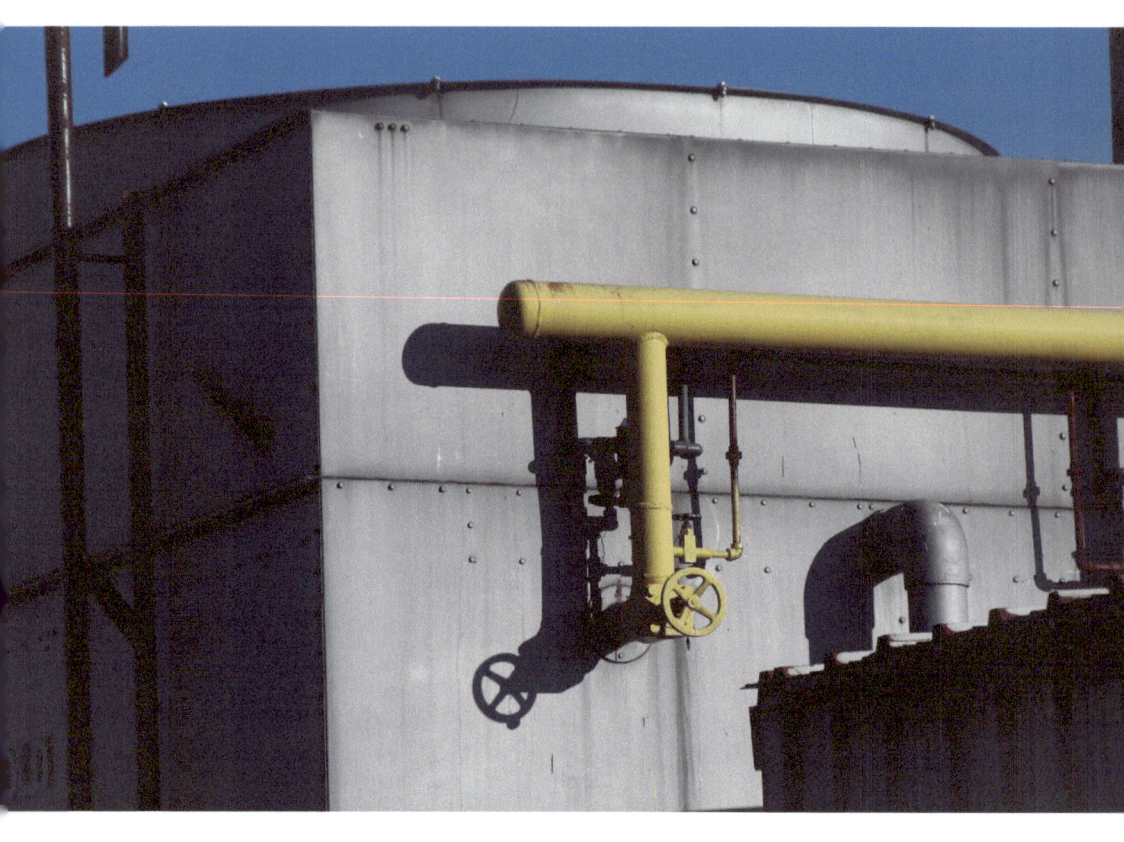

Before that, I had never heard the robin fly around the cabin making *any* kind of call, let alone a distress call. But as soon as I had that thought, I could hear the robin leave her nest and make a complete circle around the building, urgently giving her distress call as she flew.

"Okay, okay," I said. I hurriedly put on pants, a sweater and shoes and rushed into the cold morning air.

If she was so distressed that she'd leave the scene to get me to go outside, I was definitely going to help. As fast as I could.

A moment later I found why I was needed.

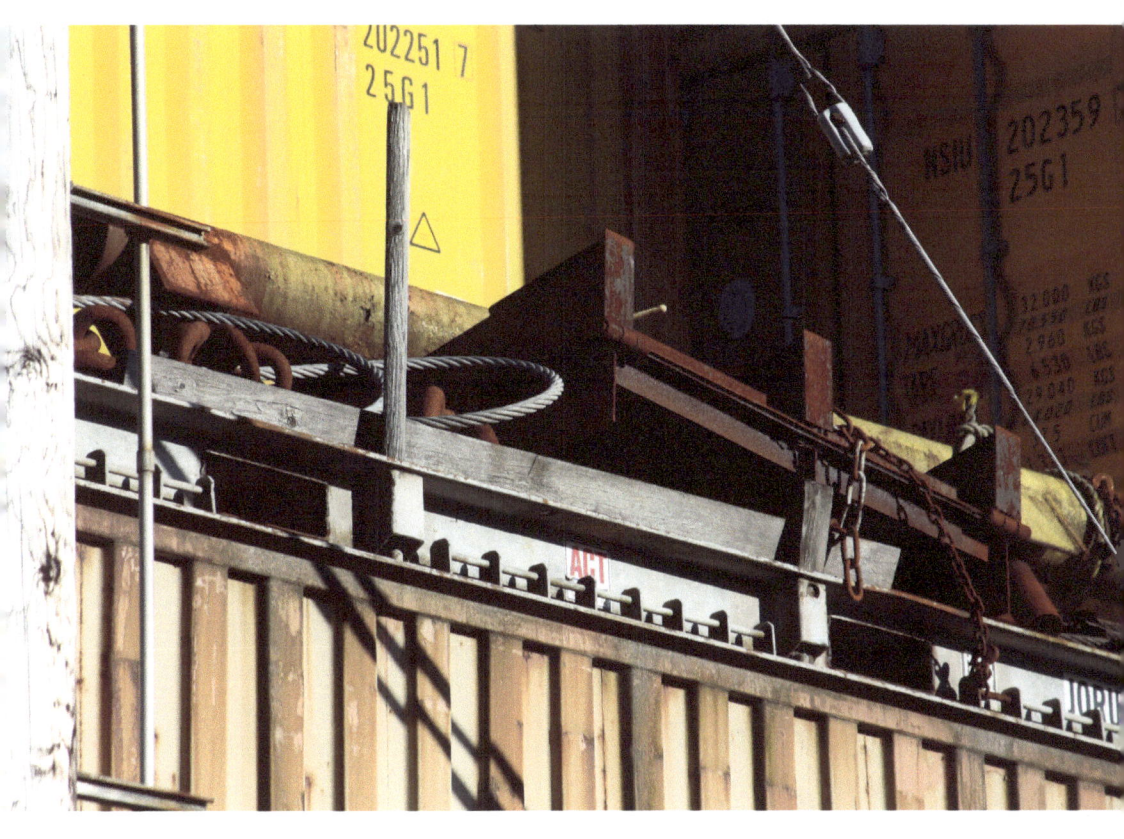

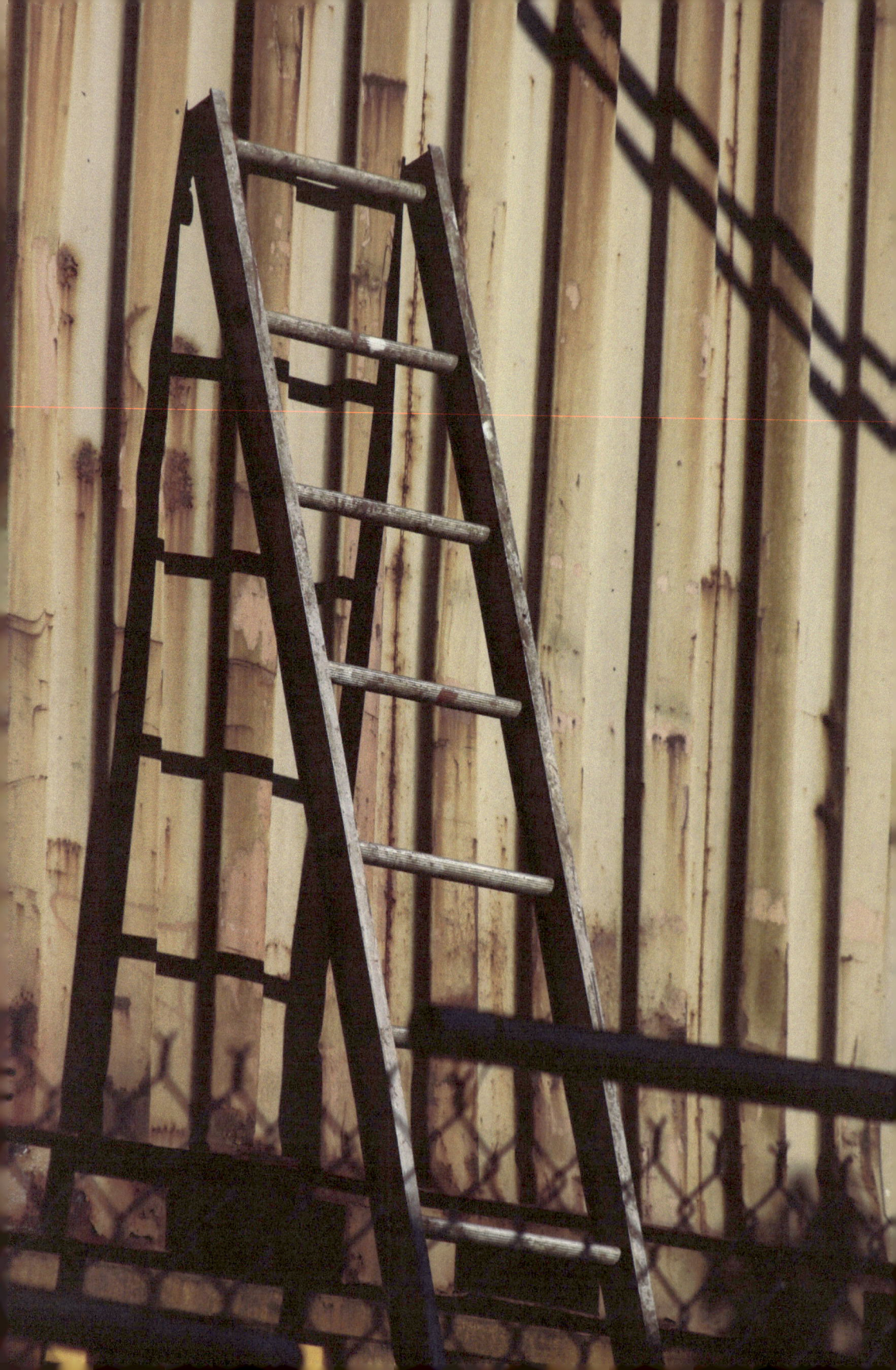

The mother robin had chosen that morning to teach her babies how to fly. The babies had made it as far as the ground, and that's where they all were – on the ground, standing and sitting, not very mobile. A few yards away, my cat, an excellent hunter, was watching with a twitching tail.

I shooed my cat away (I wasn't able to catch him that night) and went back to bed.

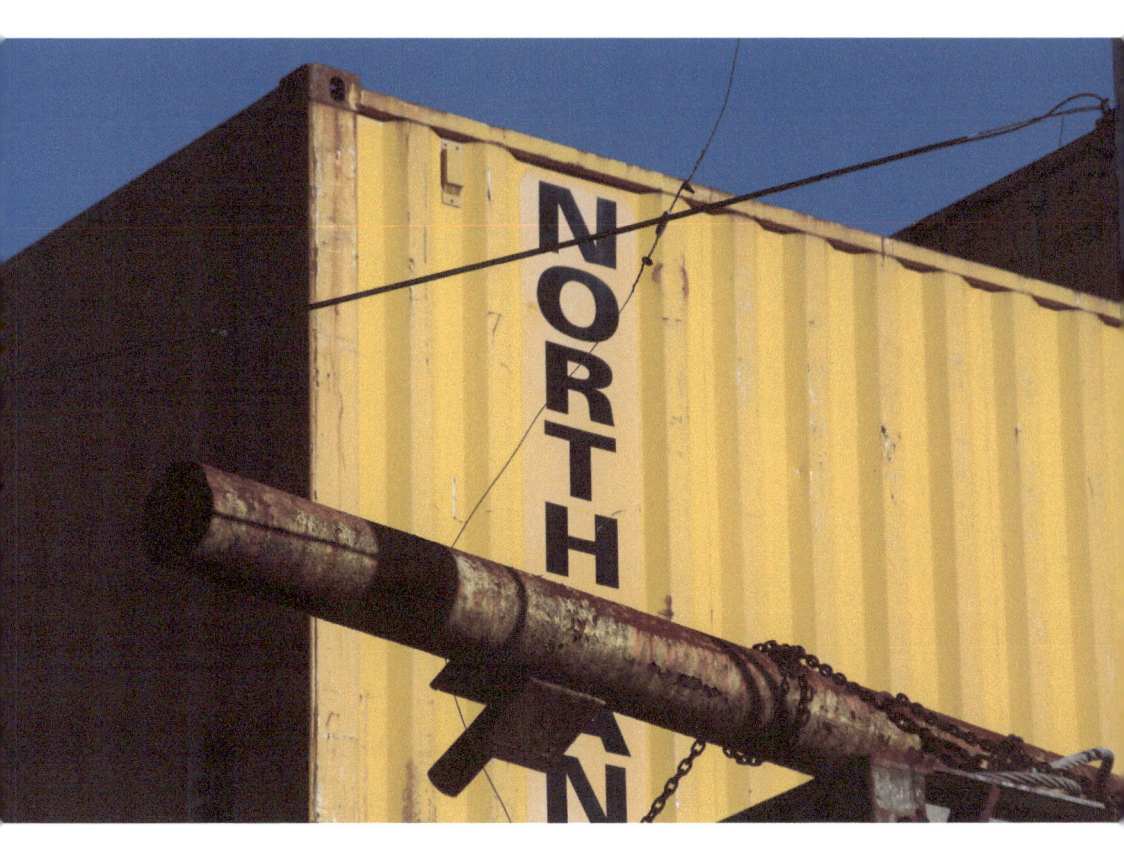

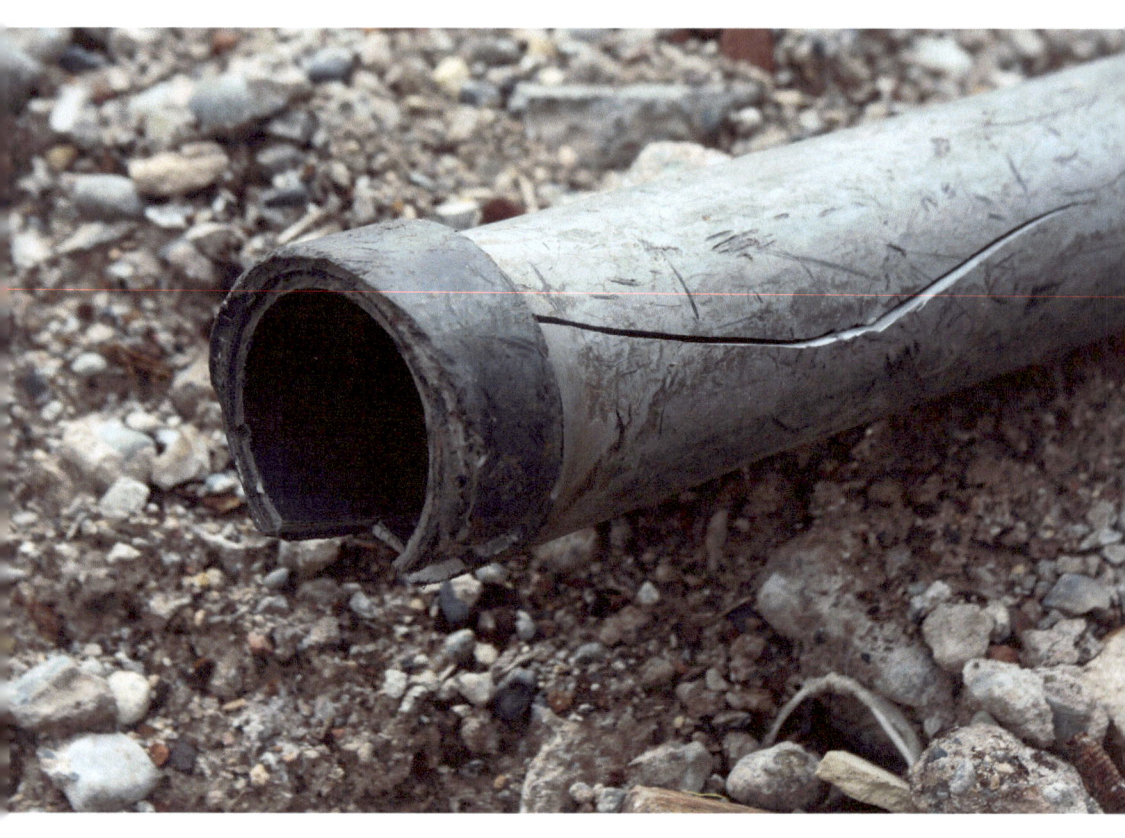

For the rest of the night, every hour until dawn, the mother robin woke me up with her distress call. Each time I got up and rescued the birds from my cat. I never did catch the cat; each time I only was able to rescue the baby birds from danger. But on the repeat times, I set no more conditions for the mother robin. She had already proved her point. I slept with my clothes on and jumped at her first call of distress and hurried out the door.

By morning there were no casualties. By then, all the babies were able to fly and get away on their own.

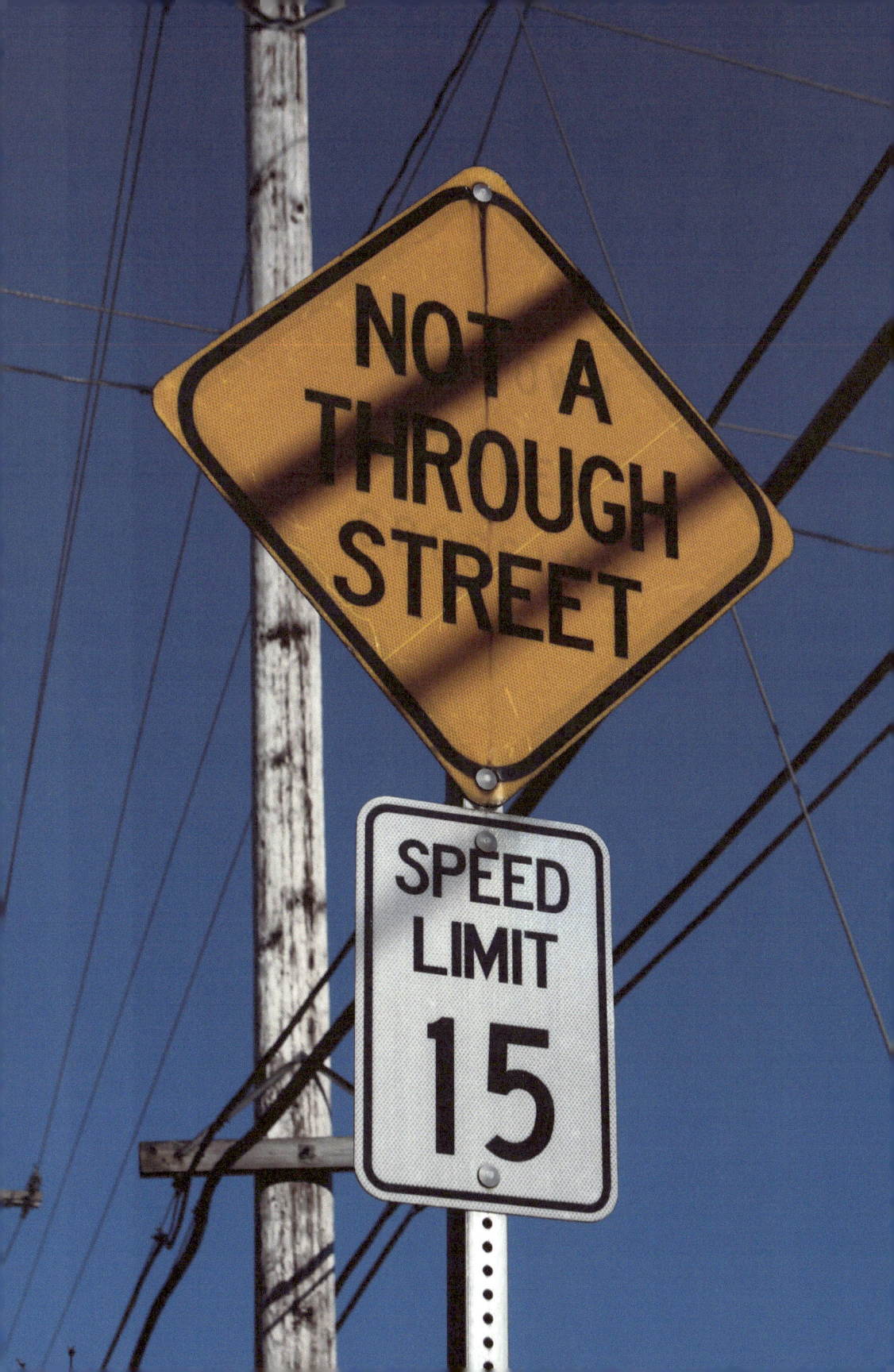

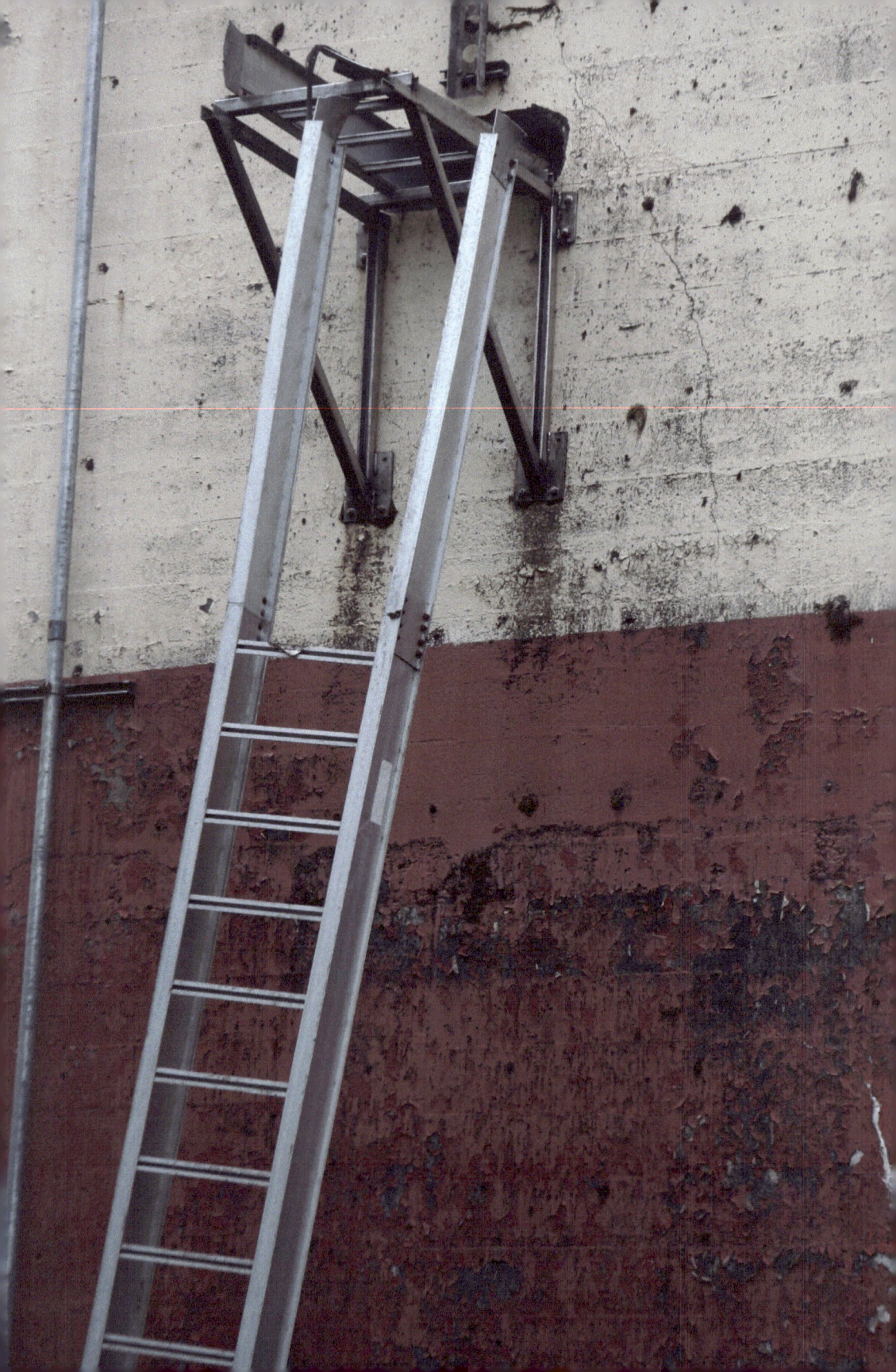

At 3 a.m. when I had thought, "I'm not getting up unless she flies around the house," it was my way of saying I planned to not get up.

But somehow the mother robin connected with my thought and acted on it. At that hour I was the only one who could rescue her babies. There was no one else within earshot; my closest neighbor was a block away.

Before the experience, I would have believed that humans and robins could communicate on some level – by gesturing with our hands we could tell them to go away, and by a tilt of their head and their song they could tell us some things about their state. But I'm not sure I would have believed that we were connected at a deeper level of understanding and that – at least in times of distress – we could communicate something as complicated as thoughts like "I'm not getting up unless you fly around the cabin" and "Okay. This is urgent."

Humans are far more connected to the environment than we realize.

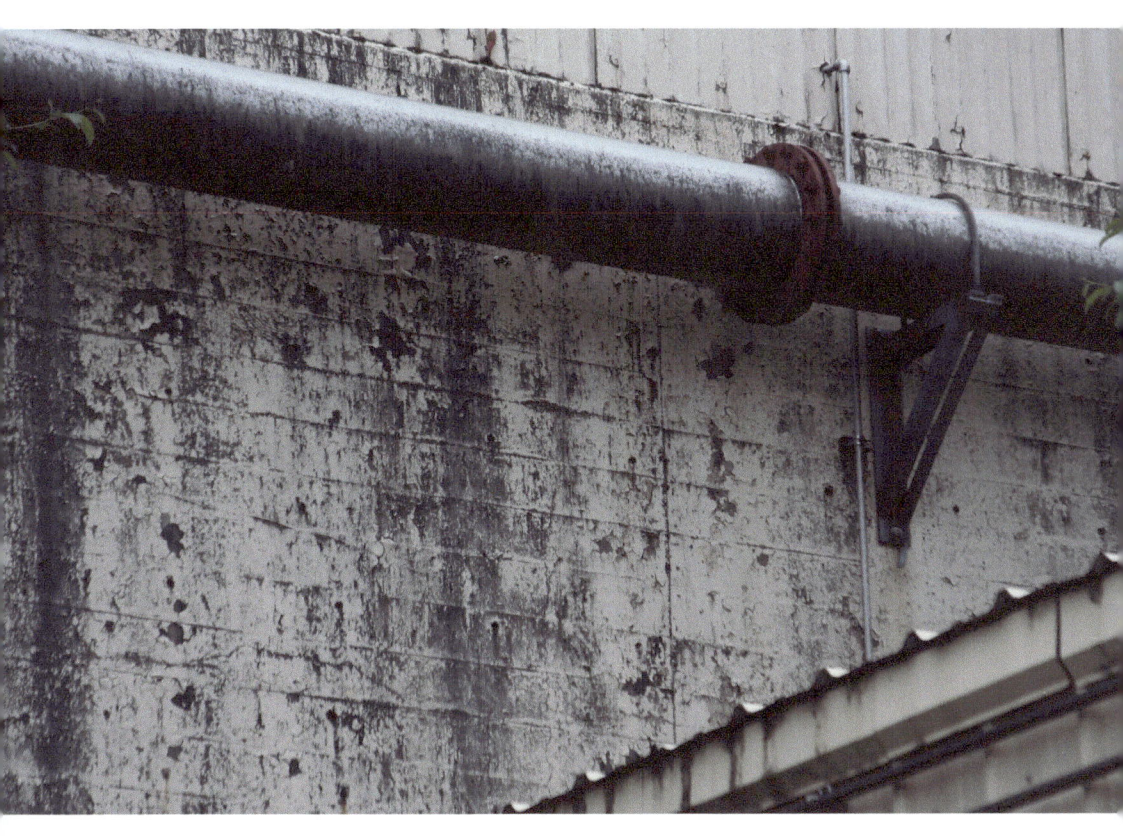

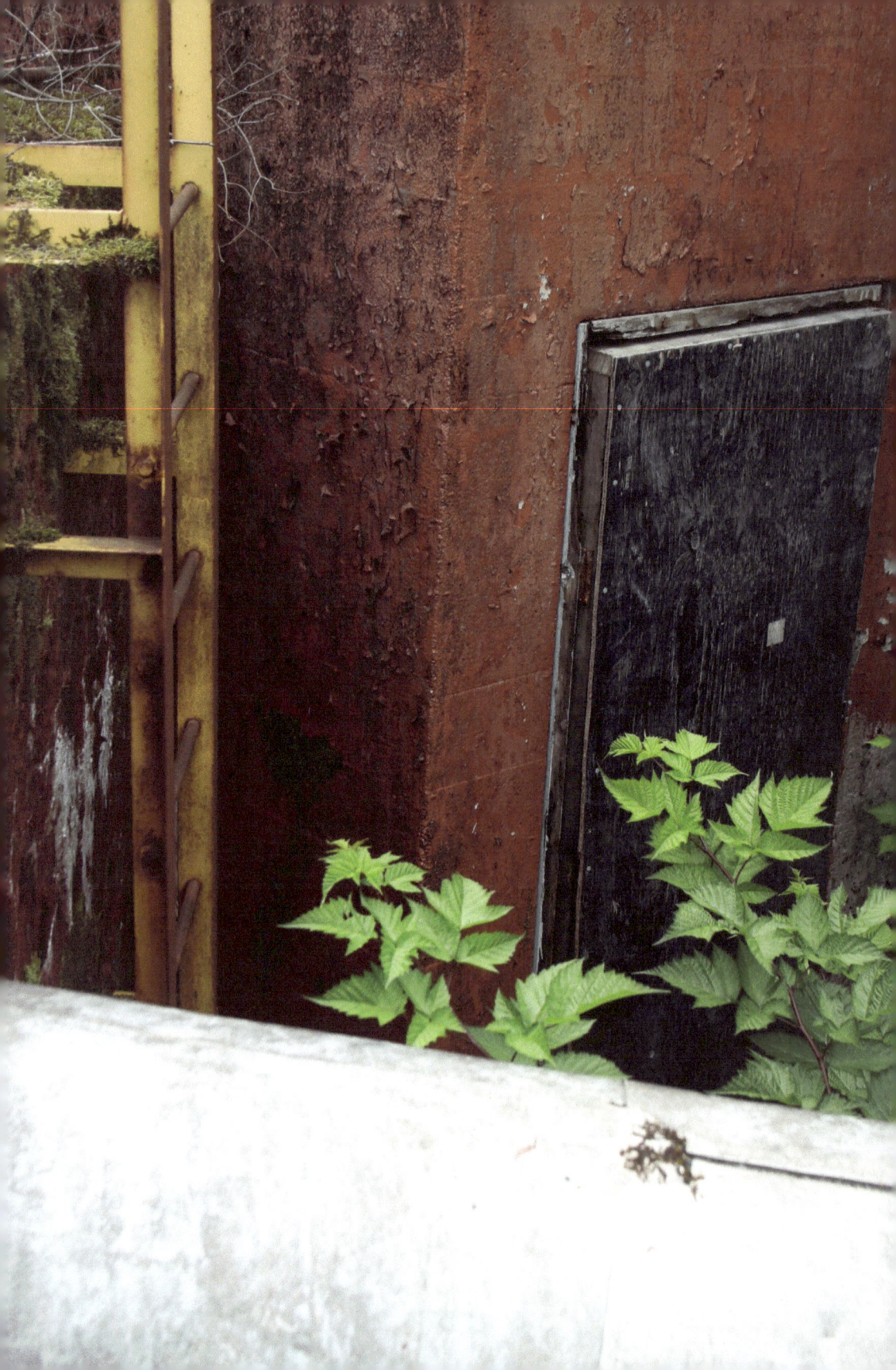

A different experience helped me see that animals are also far more connected than we think.

I was at SeaWorld in San Diego, watching the killer whales.

At least once a day the killer whales have a choreographed show. Much of the rest of the time, they're on their own.

During the show, the killer whales are fed, a reward for doing certain behaviors. Over several visits, I noticed that at least one of the killer whales kept a herring in his mouth after the show. When everyone was gone, he would spit it out, lunge for it and nab it, then spit it out again, essentially playing catch with himself.

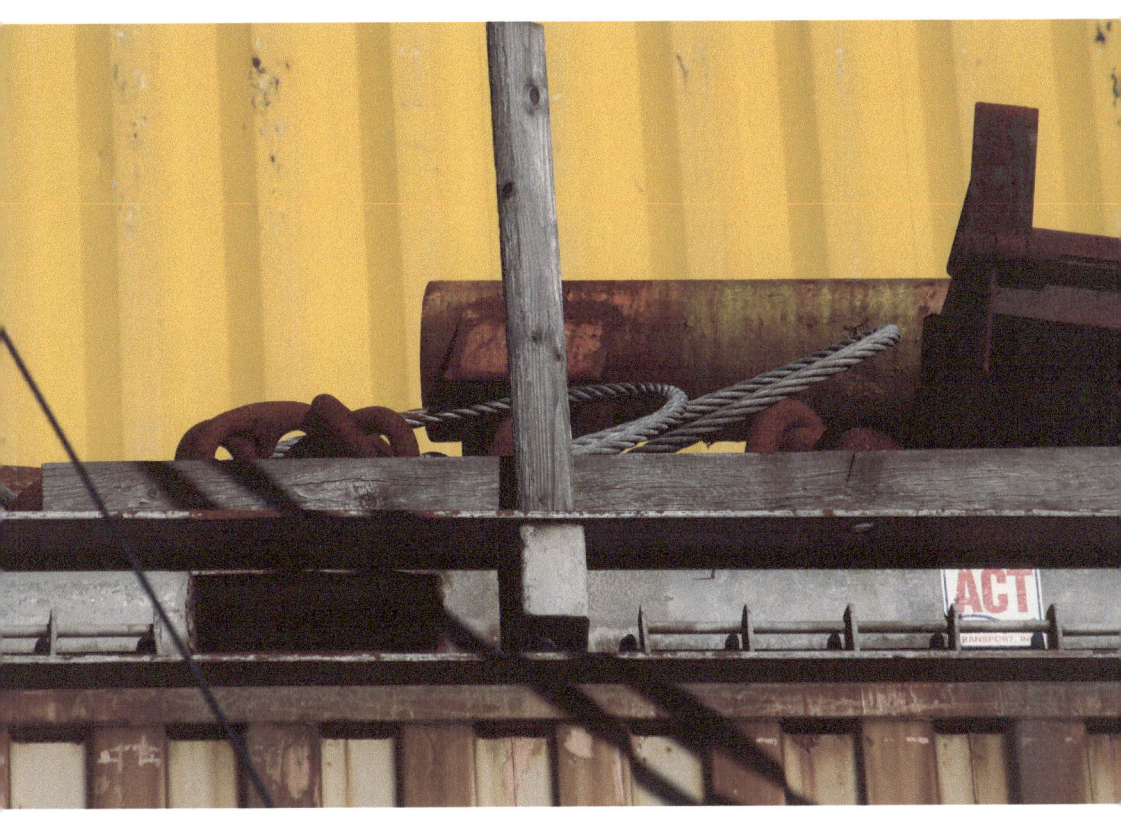

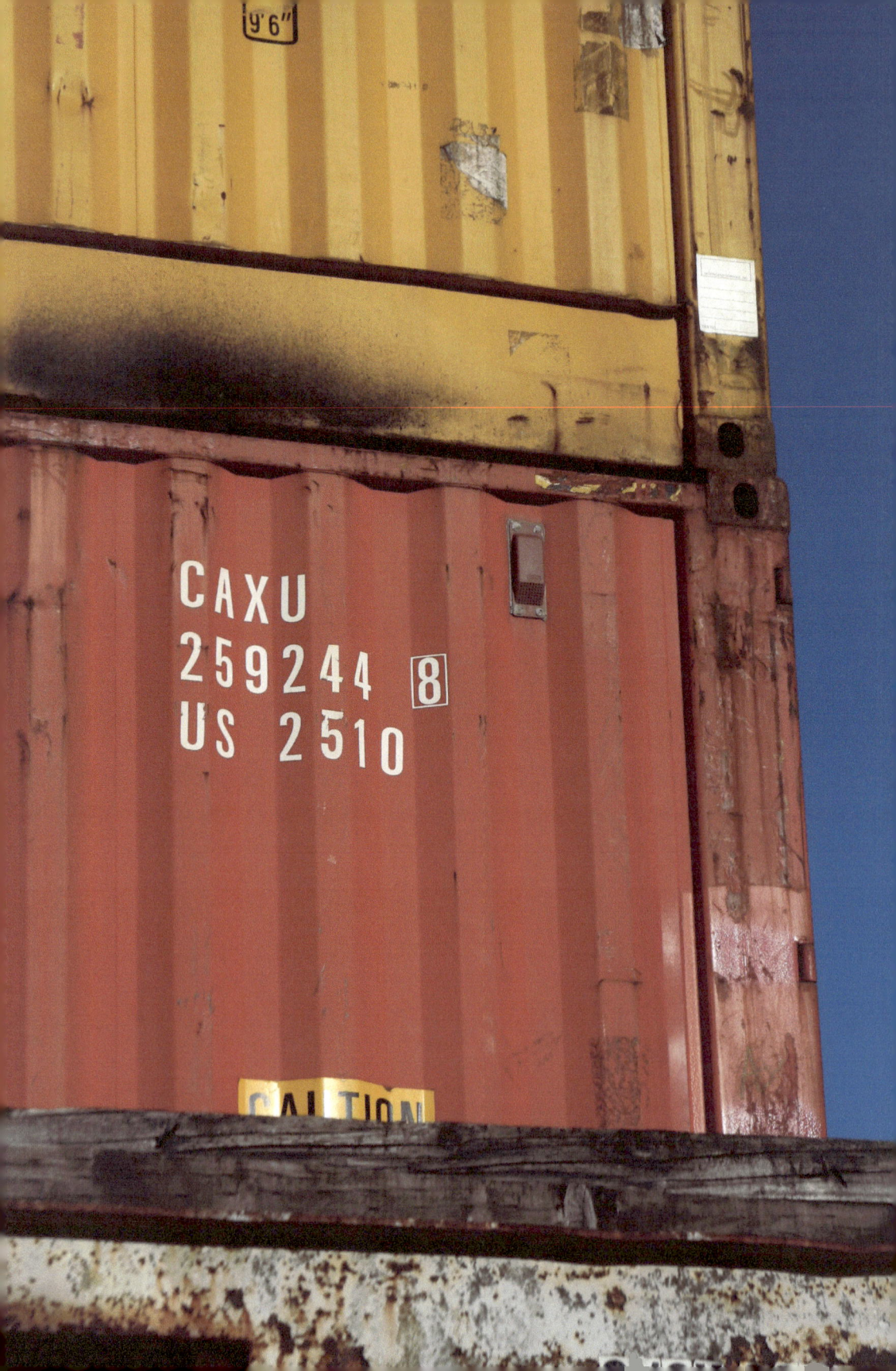

One day the rhythm was different. After he spit the herring out, he waited longer. I soon saw the reason.

A seagull flying overhead was also eyeing the herring. The killer whale would spit the herring out and wait – and wait – and wait. The killer whale wouldn't move until just before the seagull was ready to land on the herring and claim it. Then the whale would pounce on the herring. A moment later, he would spit it back out farther ahead, waiting again until the seagull was just ready to swoop in on the prize. I watched the whale and seagull do this for at least 30 minutes. The seagull never succeeded in stealing the herring.

For the next month or so, I watched this behavior over several visits.

Then one day, besides the normal seagulls flying around hoping to find food, there was a lame bird at the edge of the killer whale's tank. The bird's wing was broken, and it was unable to fly.

That day, I watched a killer whale tease a healthy seagull for awhile, always rescuing the herring and spitting it farther away whenever the seagull got too close. Then the whale swam over to the lame bird and spat the herring directly towards the bird, as if he were feeding him. The lame bird attempted to get the herring, but its broken wing made it slow, and a seagull swooped in, snagging the food. The whale came back, and spat another herring at the lame bird. This time the lame bird was able to eat.

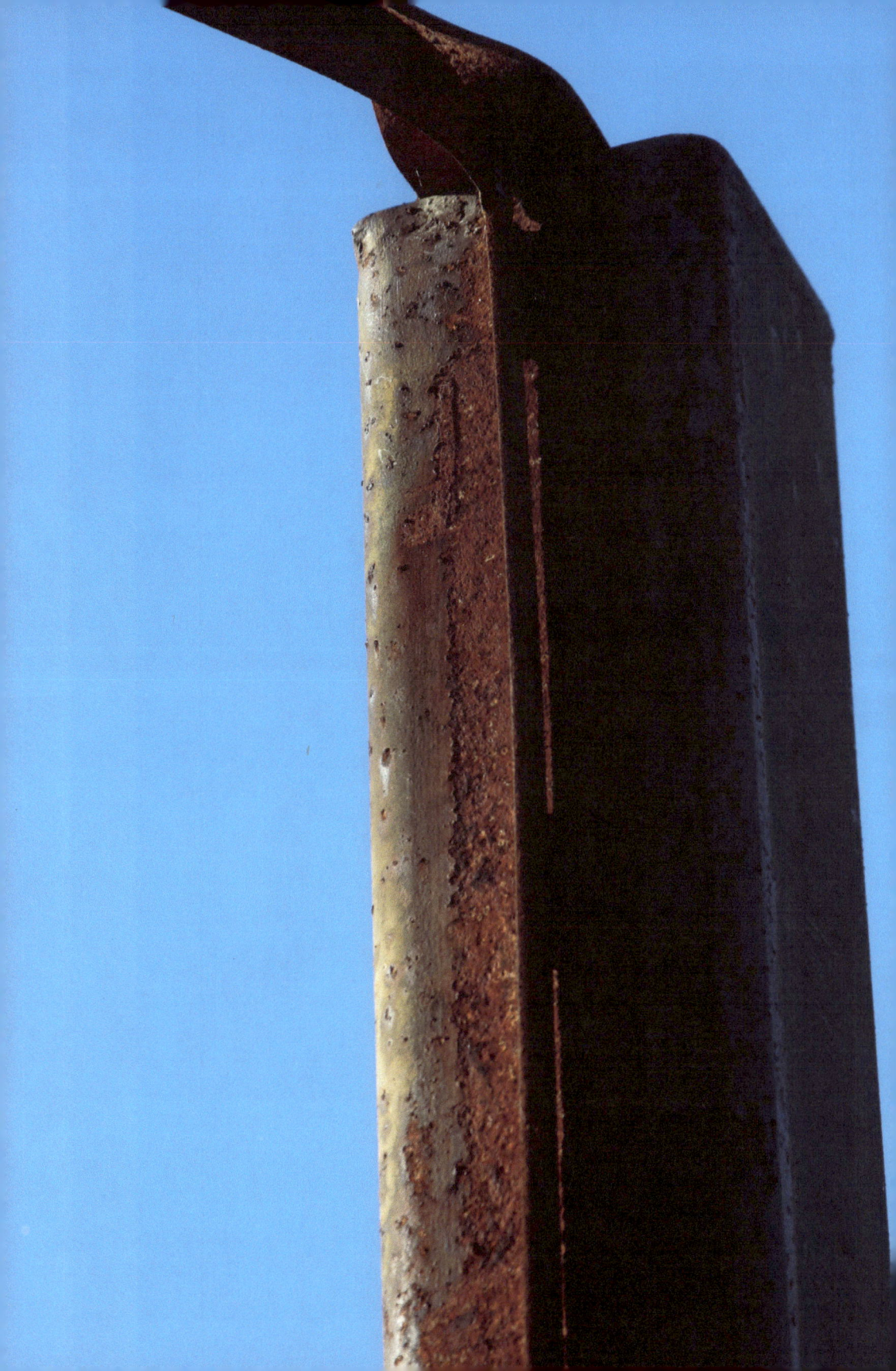

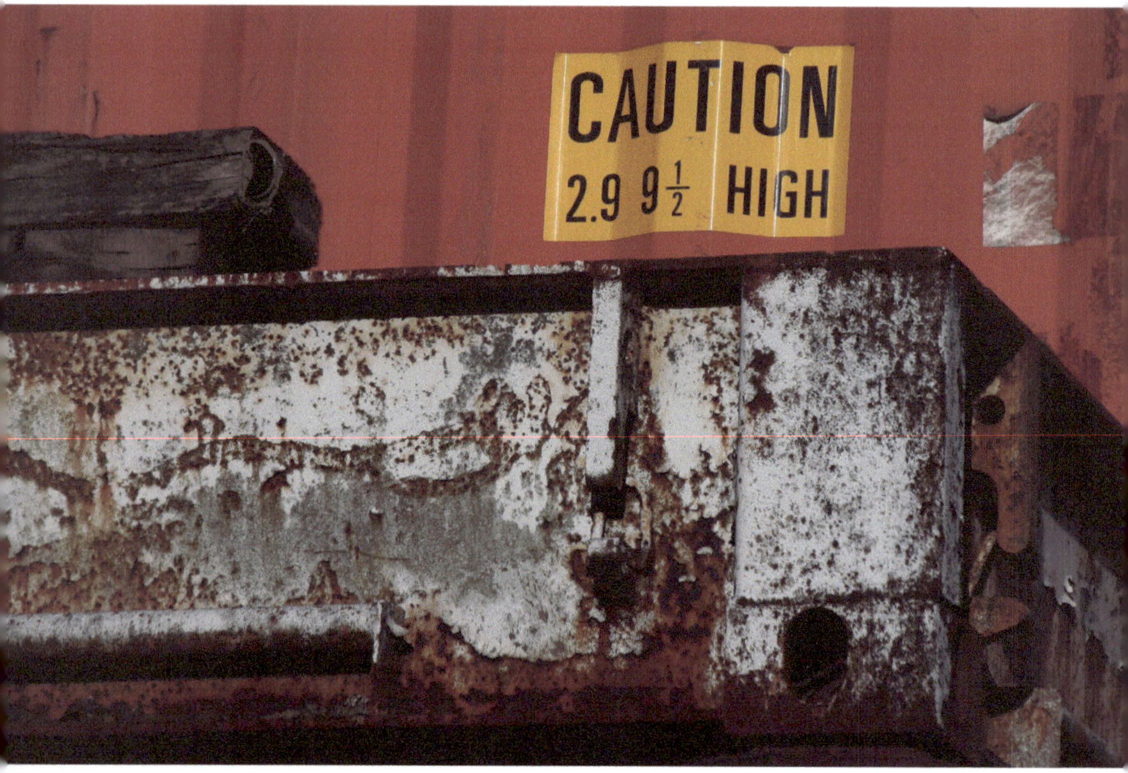

CAUTION
2.9 9½ HIGH

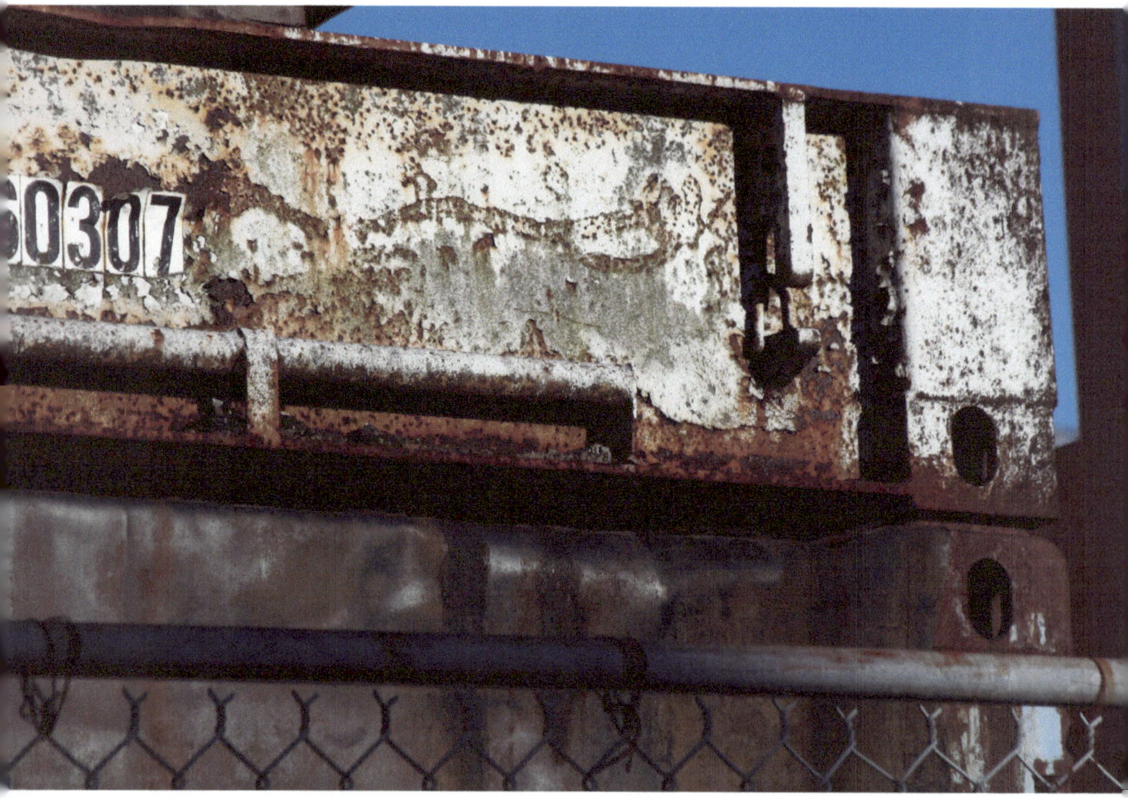

0307

If someone had told me before I watched that scene that killer whales are capable of compassion for other species, I don't know that I would have believed it. But after seeing what I saw, I don't know how else to classify it except as compassion. The killer whale saw the difference between the healthy and injured birds and responded differently. It played with (and teased) the healthy bird who could have gotten food anywhere. It helped the injured bird who couldn't get food on its own.

We are all more connected than we think.

~

Reflection question

If you believed that all creation was deeply connected, how might it change your behavior?

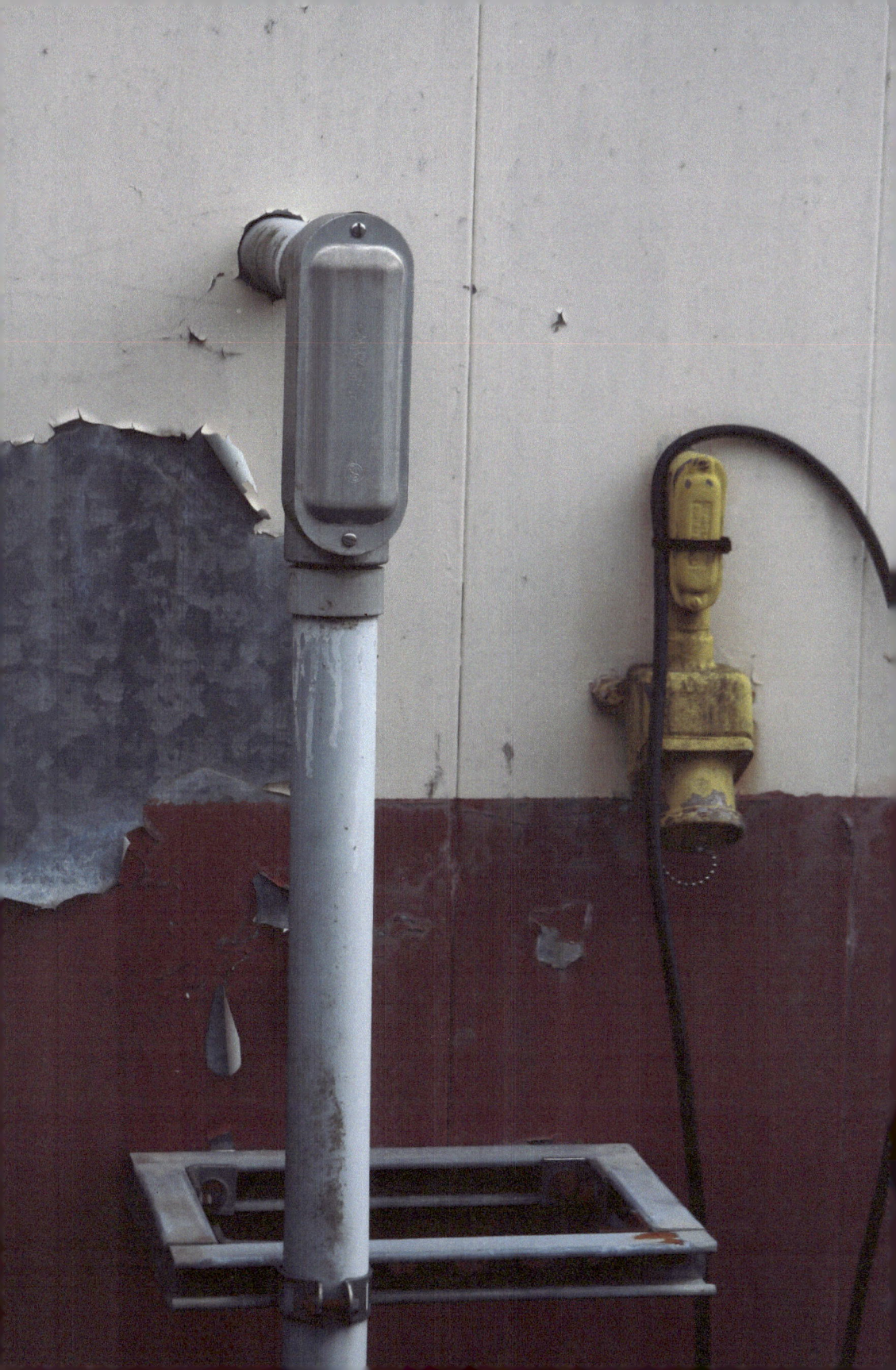

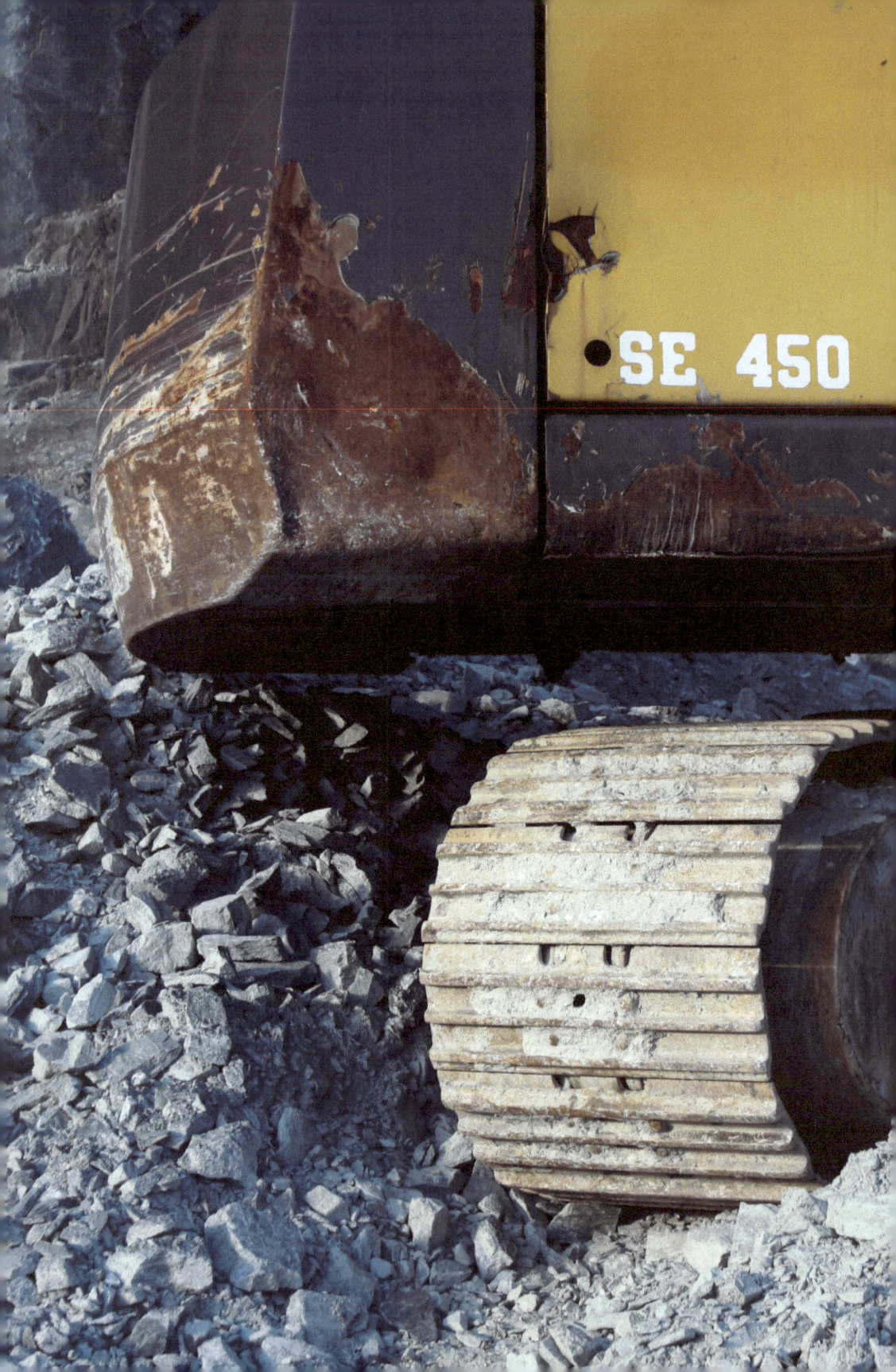

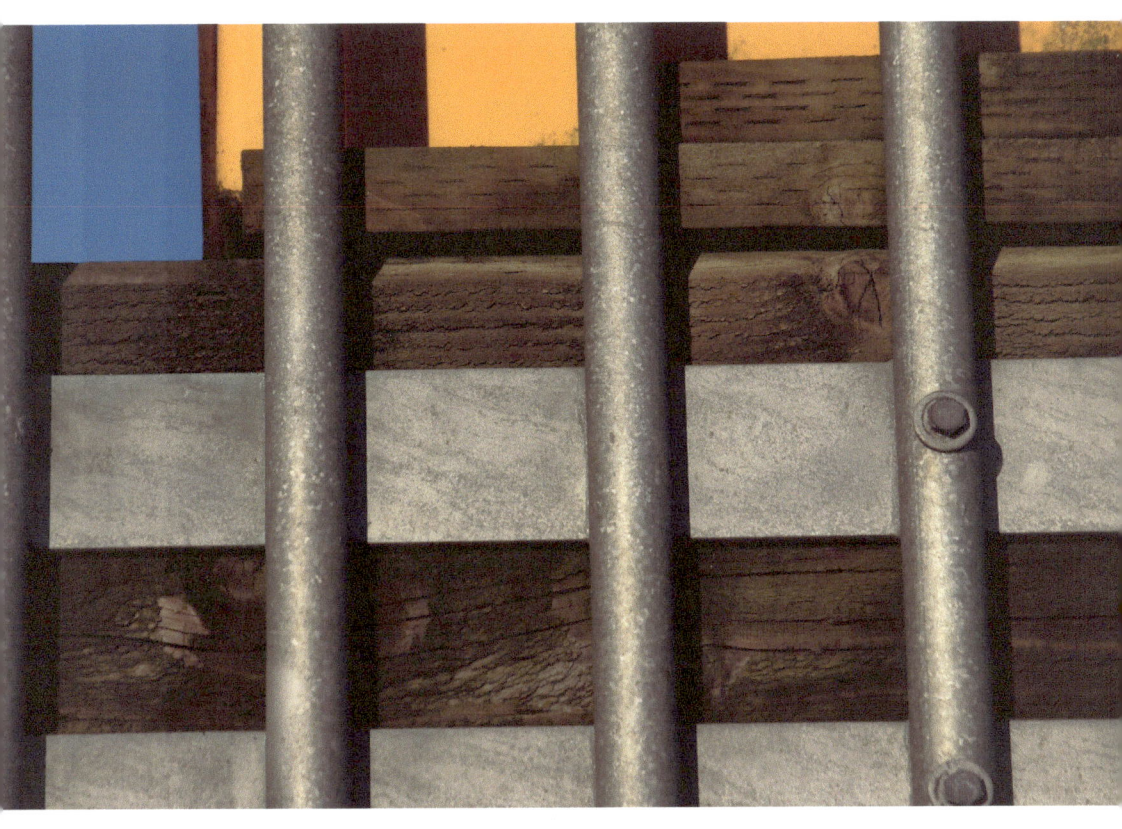

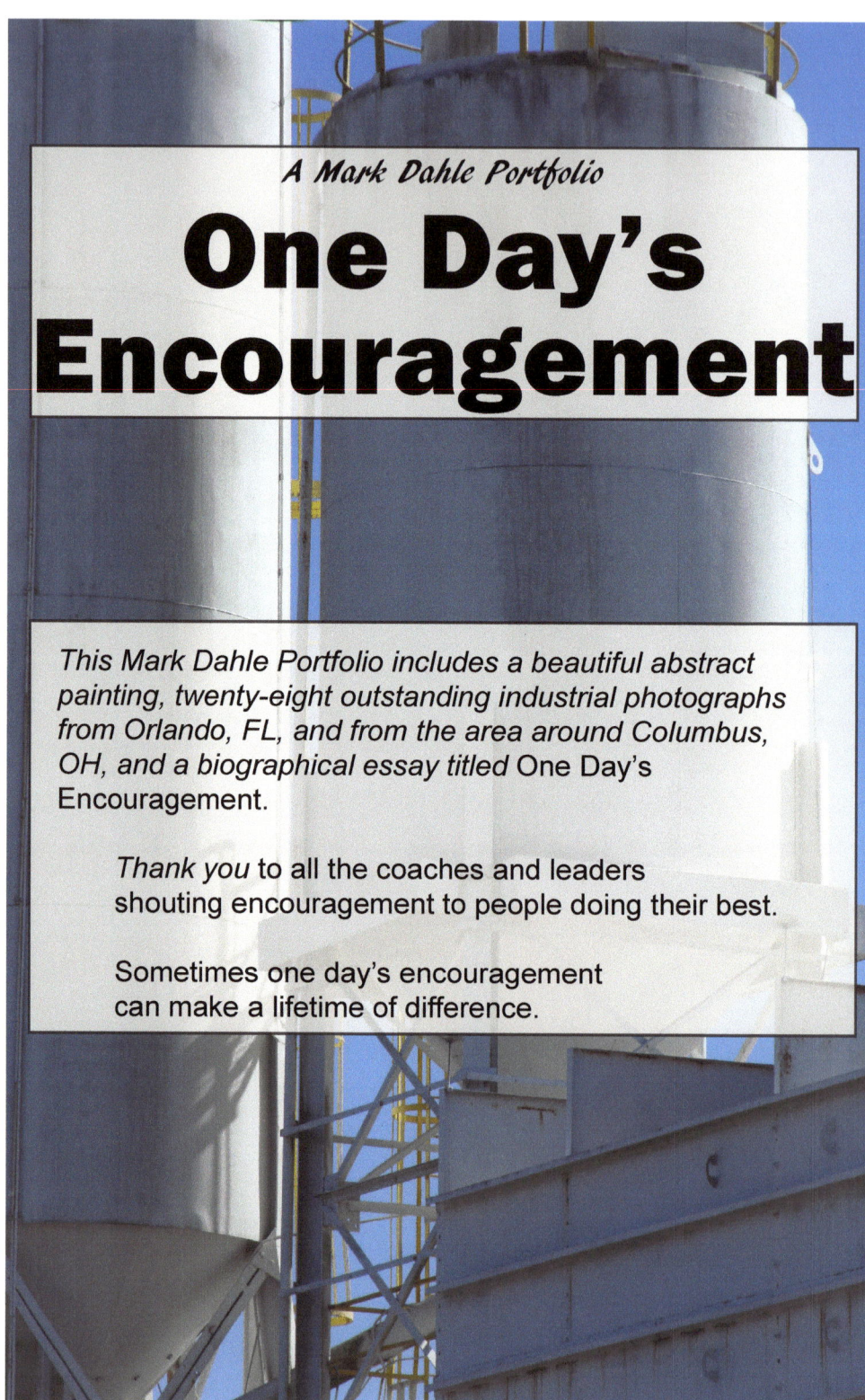

A Mark Dahle Portfolio

One Day's Encouragement

This Mark Dahle Portfolio includes a beautiful abstract painting, twenty-eight outstanding industrial photographs from Orlando, FL, and from the area around Columbus, OH, and a biographical essay titled One Day's Encouragement.

Thank you to all the coaches and leaders shouting encouragement to people doing their best.

Sometimes one day's encouragement can make a lifetime of difference.

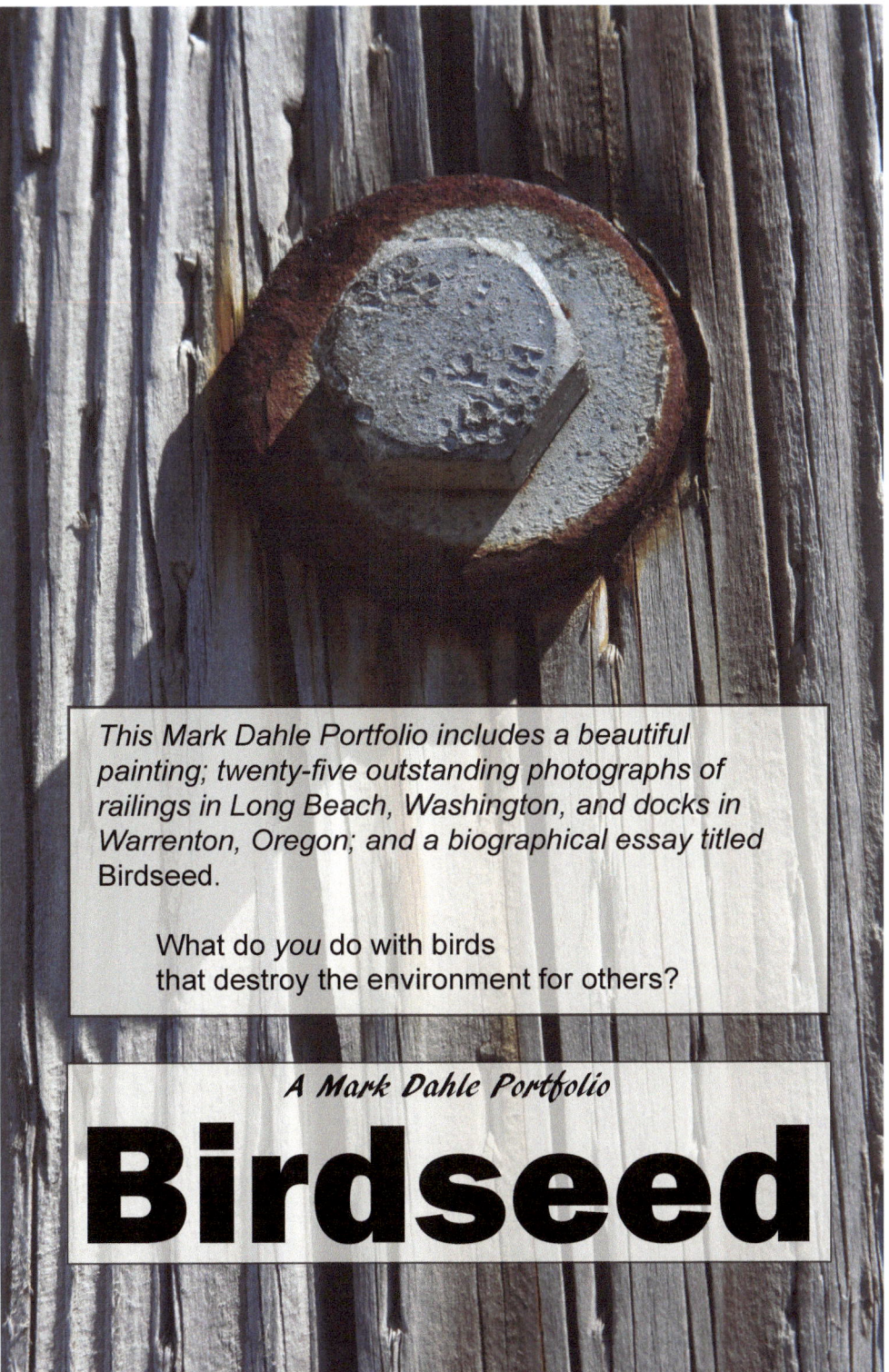

This Mark Dahle Portfolio includes a beautiful painting; twenty-five outstanding photographs of railings in Long Beach, Washington, and docks in Warrenton, Oregon; and a biographical essay titled Birdseed.

What do *you* do with birds
that destroy the environment for others?

A Mark Dahle Portfolio

Birdseed

This Mark Dahle Portfolio includes a colorful painting, twenty-eight beautiful photographs from Santa Fe and Albuquerque, New Mexico, and a narrative about Joel, who was 28.

Joel lit up a room whenever he arrived. He liked everybody, laughed easily, and was the kind of person you were glad to know. He couldn't be gone. He was too full of life.

A Mark Dahle Portfolio

Finding Joel